Original title:
The Universe Isn't Really Listening to Me

Copyright © 2025 Creative Arts Management OÜ
All rights reserved.

Author: Gideon Shaw
ISBN HARDBACK: 978-1-80566-056-9
ISBN PAPERBACK: 978-1-80566-351-5

Galactic Murmurs and Silent Cries

Stars giggle in a cosmic haze,
While I dance in my awkward ways.
Planets roll their eyes at my plea,
But who needs them? I'm just me!

A comet zooms, bright and bold,
Laughing at the tales I've told.
Constellations whisper in jest,
'Oh look, it's just another quest!'

The Vacuum of Understanding

In the vastness where silence dwells,
I send my thoughts, like ringing bells.
The black holes chuckle and spin,
While I shout out loud, 'Where do I begin?'

Galaxies swirl with their grand designs,
Yet my hopes float off like broken lines.
Gravity? More like heavy tease,
As I float in space—just aimlessly, please.

An Asteroid's Journey to Nowhere

An asteroid rolls with reckless cheer,
On a path that's nowhere near.
I wave and shout, 'Hey! Over here!'
It just shrugs, and disappears.

Orbiting dreams, but lost in flight,
The bumps and scrapes — oh what a sight!
I swerve and dodge, fulfilling none,
Just a rock that thinks it's having fun.

Unremarked Wishes Shared with the Heavens

Wishes shot like fireworks bright,
But the cosmos? Just out of sight.
I chuckle softly at my fate,
While stars blink back, 'Oh, that's great!'

A shooting star glints overhead,
It's got its own, I should be fed.
I try to chat with clouds, so high,
They puff and scoff, drifting by.

Dreams Sent adrift in the Galaxy

I whisper wishes to the stars,
They giggle back from afar.
A cosmic joke, they must have heard,
Yet silence reigns, not a single word.

Floating thoughts like comets tail,
Swirling dreams in a frantic trail.
I shout my hopes with all my might,
But they just dance in the moonlight.

Inaudible Heartbeats in the Cosmos

My heart's a drum, but no one can hear,
Echoes lost in atmospheres clear.
Stars blink down, not a care to spare,
While I do cartwheels in cosmic glare.

I send out signals in Morse code flashes,
Yet planets chuckle, as silence crashes.
Galaxies twirl, they twist and they spin,
While I'm here waiting—let the show begin!

Particle Poetry in a Silent Sphere

I pen my rhymes on a cosmic sheet,
But quarks just giggle, they can't take the heat.
I declare my lines with flair and grace,
Still, they remain with a poker face.

Einstein smiles at my plight so keen,
While atoms snicker from the unseen.
I toss verses like seeds in voided air,
Ah, the joy of writing—a cosmic affair!

Stardust Thoughts in a Void of Silence

Collecting thoughts like scattered dust,
I launch them out, in dreams I trust.
Stars pretend they're struck by awe,
While giggling softly at my faux pas.

I craft a tale of light years, bold,
Yet meteors chuckle at the stories told.
With every giggle from black holes round,
I realize hoots and hollers abound.

A Halting Heartbeat Amidst the Cosmic Flow

I sent my wishes on a star,
But my wishes just seemed too far.
The cosmos giggled in delight,
While I pondered my last late-night bite.

I yelled my dreams into the sky,
A comet just zoomed by.
Did it hear me? Not a chance,
It was off to a galactic dance.

I tried to talk to the moon,
But it just hummed a tuneless tune.
Amongst the dust and glowing light,
I figured I'd lost my cosmic fight.

So here I stand with half a grin,
Chasing echoes of where I've been.
In the vastness, I'll take a stance,
And laugh at my own cosmic dance.

The Unheard Dialogue with Infinity

I asked the stars for a sign or clue,
But all I got was a twinkling view.
I waved my arms and called out loud,
They just sparkled, forming a crowd.

I thought I'd reason with a distant sun,
It winked at me—was that a pun?
As I rambled on about my plight,
It seemed too busy for a friendly light.

I tried to share my coffee break,
But black holes just made me ache.
They gulped down all my witty tales,
As I drifted off in cosmic gales.

Creating friendships with the void,
My chatter left them all annoyed.
Yet in this silence, I find some glee,
For maybe madness is the key to be free.

Stars that Glisten, Yet Do Not Listen

Twinkling in the night sky bright,
They sparkle, dance, and tease my sight.
I shout, 'Hey stars, can you hear me?'
They snicker softly, 'Oh, just let it be.'

Hoping for a cosmic reply,
They wink and shine as I sigh.
'What's the deal?' I ask in jest,
They giggle back, 'We're just here for the rest.'

In the Shadow of Soaring Nebulae

Beneath the clouds of cosmic dust,
I ponder dreams but feel nonplussed.
Oh great nebulae, hear my plea,
'Why can't you just pay attention to me?'

They swirl and play in colors bright,
Ignoring me in their dizzy flight.
I swear I saw a star roll its eye,
As I complained with a cosmic sigh.

Whispers Carried by a Cosmic Breeze

I shout my secrets to the void,
The winds just laugh, they're so overjoyed.
With every gust, they swirl and tease,
My worries float off with utmost ease.

I thought they'd catch my heartfelt tone,
But space just grins—I'm not alone.
A comet zips by, gives me a grin,
'Your thoughts, my friend, are lost in the spin!'

A Harmony of Light, Unmatched by Sound

In the stillness, I tap a beat,
An echo of hope, oh so sweet.
Yet silence reigns beyond my plea,
As planets chuckle, 'Just let it be!'

A symphony, I think I hear,
But it's just the void, far and near.
Each twinkling light, a playful jest,
In this grand game, I'm just a guest.

Celestial Dreams and Distant Silence

I shout at stars, they sparkle bright,
Yet my wishes float into the night.
A comet whizzes by, with a cheeky grin,
As if to say, "Oh, where to begin?"

I speak to planets, they spin away,
In their grand ballet, they won't stay.
A moonbeam giggles, lighting my face,
While I'm left here, not finding my place.

Galaxies swirl, chasing their tails,
While I'm tossing rhymes like paper sails.
"Hello!" I holler, to a black hole,
It just swallows sound, plays its role.

Yet I can't help but laugh at this dance,
Chasing echoes of a cosmic chance.
In this silent show with no one to see,
I'm the lone jester in the galaxy.

Universes Away: A Quiet Reflection

I pen my dreams into the void,
Hoping for chuckles, but I'm just toyed.
A supernova's spark, oh what a tease,
It's like they're laughing, with cosmic leaves.

Stars hold meetings, I'm not on the list,
While I'm shouting wishes, shaking my fist.
A swirl of colors, but here I sit,
Caught in the silence, not a word fit.

Black holes guffaw with their tricky charms,
As I wave my arms, playing my shams.
Planets go waltzing, in a starry dream,
But they never notice my silent scream.

Reflecting on adventures that never took flight,
I jest with the cosmos, not feeling quite slighted.
In this grand jest, I find my own peace,
Though the universe giggles, my sighs never cease.

When the Cosmos Ignores My Call

I dial the stars, but no one picks up,
It's like they're sipping tea from a golden cup.
I yell, I giggle, offer a snack,
But they just twinkle, and that's the facts.

Shooting stars zoom past, in a hurry way,
"C'mon, listen up!" I want to say.
A planetary friend gives a nonchalant wave,
While I'm caught in this cosmic enclave.

I tickle asteroids, hoping for sound,
But they just bounce off, round and round.
Amidst the silence, I make a toast,
To the distant realms that ignore my boast.

Still, in this chaos, I find some delight,
As I dance with silence, through the night.
Even when ignored, I'll play my part,
A joyful fool with an unyielding heart.

Galactic Echoes of an Unheard Heart

I send my thoughts to the Milky Way,
But they get lost in the cosmic ballet.
With meteors racing and quasars bright,
I laugh at my whispers that fade in the light.

The cosmos plays coy, what a funny game,
While I wear my heart like a badge of fame.
I wave at the nebula, it winks at me,
Yet doesn't respond, how rude can it be?

A dance of galaxies twirls all around,
In this silent party, I make not a sound.
My lonely heart flutters while they rejoice,
I whirl in my solitude and laugh at my voice.

Yet I'll keep on talking to the stars up high,
In cosmic banter beneath the vast sky.
For even when the echoes depart,
I'm still the dreamer with a joyful heart.

Distant Realities

I shout my thoughts to silent skies,
The comets wink, ignore my cries.
I dance beneath their cosmic show,
They laugh, I'm just a little show.

Galaxies swirl in swirling cheer,
My grand ideas can't reach their sphere.
I plot my schemes, but they just yawn,
Stardust dreams by break of dawn.

Absent Attention

Oh, how I search for signs up there,
But all I see is empty air.
I wave my hands in cosmic glee,
A black hole giggles back at me.

The planets spin, they've got no care,
Ignoring me, their cosmic flair.
I try to find a friend in space,
But every star just turns its face.

When Lightyears Separate Soul and Star

My wishes fly on starlit beams,
But reach the stars, they burst my dreams.
I pen my hopes on meteor trails,
Yet all I get are giant fails.

While planets frolic, gleaming bright,
I'm left to spin in endless night.
I ask for wisdom from the moon,
It shrugs and hums a distant tune.

While Stars Spin, I Remain Ignored

A cosmic talk show, but I'm not there,
The stars are busy, they never care.
I bring my popcorn, all prepared,
But in their brilliance, I'm just scared.

The sun just giggles, shining bold,
While I'm left out in the cold.
I try to join their dazzling games,
But they're too busy, sounding their names.

Skimming Silences of Starlit Dreams

In cosmic whispers, I try to speak,
But it's just silence, what a freak!
I toss my hopes to shooting stars,
They dodge my wishes, leaving scars.

While nebulae dance in vibrant hues,
I'm lost in my own silly blues.
I chase the echoes, where do they go?
The cosmos chuckles, 'You should know!'

Whispers Lost in Stardust

I shout to the stars, but they just twinkle,
My jokes fall flat, like a cosmic crinkle.
A black hole laughs, just sucking it in,
While comets glide past, never a grin.

The planets are spinning, in their own dance,
My cosmic complaints are lost at a glance.
I ponder aloud, with no one to hear,
Even space dust just drifts, without a cheer.

I ask for a sign, a wink or a nod,
But they all seem busy, just laying the cod.
And while I sit here, feeling absurd,
Even starlight ignores my heartfelt word.

So I'll keep on talking, though I know it's vain,
To echoes of silence, I'll entertain.
Because maybe one day, when I'm feeling spry,
A quasar will chuckle, or at least we might try.

The Indifference of Celestial Bodies

Oh Moon, my friend, you're so far away,
You never reply, not a word to say.
I toss up my thoughts, they go straight to dust,
You bask in your glow, in celestial lust.

Dear Sun, shining bright, do you even care?
I wave my arms wildly, you're always elsewhere.
With all of that heat, can't you give me a wink?
Instead, you just burn while I sit here to think.

Mars rolls its eyes, in its rusty red mode,
With craters and dust, it's too tired to load.
While Jupiter's swirling, with its great big storm,
I'm left with my laughter, just looking for warmth.

And Saturn, dear friend, with those rings so grand,
You're too busy spinning, or stuck in the sand.
So I'll chatter to nothing, forever I'll cling,
To thoughts of your silence, as I laugh and sing.

In the Shadow of a Distant Sun

In the shadow of stars, I'm here with my thoughts,
Conversations with nothing, they tie me in knots.
The blackness surrounds me, it giggles and sways,
While I send my wishes in whimsical ways.

I ask for a dance from a meteor sprite,
But they glance then zoom off, into the night.
The cosmos just sighs, a big yawning breeze,
I'm talking to nothing, it's all just a tease.

I toss my ideas, they float like the dust,
Yet no cosmic audience, it's like I'm unjust.
A sigh from a comet, a twinkle, then gone,
And I'm left with my laughter, alone on the lawn.

The echoes of silence, they chuckle with glee,
While I joke with the void, expecting a spree.
Yet here in the shadows, I'll dance with delight,
With my witty remarks, and my humor in flight.

Conversations with Darkness

In the depths of the night, I'm chatting away,
To shadows and whispers that brightly display.
They don't have a voice, but I'm sure they know,
All my punchlines land with a comedic flow.

I crack cosmic jokes, but the darkness just sighs,
Fluffy clouds giggle, but I don't know why.
I plead with the void for a titter or cheer,
But instead, I get silence — it's painfully clear.

I ask for a punchline from the great Milky Way,
But it only twirls, not a word to say.
Even black holes don't giggle at humor divine,
They just suck it all in, while I sit here and pine.

So I'll keep conversing, and who knows, maybe one,
Day the stars will reply with a radiant pun.
Till then I'm just laughing, where starlight is dark,
In the shadows of silence, I still hit my mark.

When Silence Speaks Louder than Stars

In the night, I shout to the sky,
But all I get back is a sigh.
The moons laugh, the comets tease,
While I talk to them like they've got keys.

I asked for signs in a cosmic dance,
They winked, I thought it was my chance.
But it's just crickets, chirping away,
Like they're off on a galactic holiday.

I sent a postcard to the Big Dipper,
But I guess my address was a little slippy.
Light years are tricky, my messages fade,
Do they find my humor? Or are they just swayed?

So here I sit, beneath the dome,
Chatting with shadows that call me home.
I crack the jokes, but they never reply,
Maybe stars just prefer the high and dry.

Distant Dreams in a Cold Expanse

With big dreams stretching across the night,
I threw my wishes, oh what a sight!
But they floated off like balloons in a breeze,
And now I'm left here, lost in the freeze.

The galaxies giggle at my attempts,
While I ponder over star maps, in pretense.
I once tried to dance, but tripped on a star,
Now I'm just a meme, on a comet, bizarre.

My phone is silent, though I text the sky,
Perhaps it's busy—did I reply?
I thought we were pals, but I guess I was wrong,
Now I'm spinning alone in a cosmic song.

I brewed some coffee to drink with Mars,
But he's too busy with his flashy cars.
So here I am, alone with my thoughts,
Telling the cosmos my lonely plots.

Stardust Messages Fall Silent

I wrote my dreams in shimmering dust,
Hoping they'd pierce through the velvet crust.
But the meteors whizzed on their merry way,
Ignoring my plight like I was cliché.

I sent a wish tied to a comet's tail,
But it got sidetracked, like a snail.
If wishes were whispers in a celestial race,
Mine got lost in the vacuum of space.

I scribbled notes in the Milky Way,
But got feedback that took me astray.
The stars just twinkled with dubious glee,
As if my shenanigans were comedy.

Now I shout at the sky, a one-man show,
As silent stardust drifts down, slow.
The cosmos chuckles, what's next, my friend?
I'll just sit here and wait for the end.

Silent Stars Overheard

I caught a glimpse of a curious star,
Thought it might want to travel far.
But its light flickered like an old TV,
And I realized it's not really into me.

I whispered sweet nothings to a passing glow,
But it turned out to be a UFO show.
So now I'm out here, feeling quite silly,
Talking to voids while they just giggle freely.

The sun rolled its eyes, the moons just yawned,
As I poured my heart out, a little less fawned.
Did I really think they cared for my plight?
They're too busy orbiting, day and night!

So I'll keep babbling in this cosmic soup,
While quasars laugh and jump through the loop.
Maybe someday they'll drop in for tea,
But for now, it's just me and my comedy.

Floating Thoughts in a Silent Space

In a vacuum, my ideas drift,
Like balloons lost in a gust.
I shout at the cosmos with a grin,
They just twinkle back, nonplussed.

Asteroids roll past with a laugh,
Stars giggle at my grand plans.
I thought I'd find a cosmic muse,
Instead, I'm left talking to cans.

Galaxies spin, they've got their own show,
While I float here, a quirk on repeat.
I scribble my thoughts on stardust waves,
In this silence, I can't find my beat.

Yet I chuckle, waving my arms wide,
To the void that never replies.
Or maybe it's just a cosmic prank,
And I'm the punchline in the skies.

Chasing Echoes in a Starlit Sea

I call to the stars, oh-so-sweet,
But they echo back, lost in their play.
'Hello!' I cheer, to the endless night,
Yet the twinkle responds, 'Save it for day.'

Waves of light splash against my cheek,
As I chase shadows of a distant glow.
The jokes are dry in this grand expanse,
Like missing socks in a cosmic throw.

Ranked among comets who all just flee,
With a punchline I can't seem to find.
The laughter of space is a distant tune,
While I mumble to black holes left behind.

But still I sail on this silky sea,
Listening for chuckles in void's embrace.
If the cosmos won't laugh with me, oh well,
I'll content myself with stars in my face.

The Unseen Dialogues with Eternity

I talk to infinity, it stays aloof,
With a twinkle it rolls its unseen eyes.
I ask deep questions, like 'What's the scoop?'
Yet all I get back are distant sighs.

Time walks by with a casual stride,
While I trip over thoughts like space debris.
'Am I a cosmic jester?' I bellow wide,
But eternity just shrugs, and says, 'We'll see.'

The planets spin tales I can't comprehend,
Bantering secrets I'm bound to miss.
If they're gossiping right up to the end,
I'm concocting my own cosmic bliss.

So here I stand, with my quirky schtick,
Hoping for giggles between the stars.
In the dance of the dark, I'm the punchline pic,
To eternity's jokes and absurd memoirs.

Stars Blink, I Whisper

Stars wink at me from their velvet veil,
I whisper sweet nothings, but they don't care.
Gazing in awe at their shimmering tail,
While I pretend my musings are rare.

I jot down my notes on the night's skin,
Hoping some stardust might fall on my page.
But even the meteors just grin,
As if my thoughts are a cosmic stage.

Poke the sky with my wild, little dreams,
Yet the comets just sneeze, sending dust.
They flutter away while I moonwalk schemes,
Smitten by starlight, a celestial trust.

Nonetheless, I giggle at all that I say,
In the silence, where echoes just dance.
While I converse with the grand Milky Way,
It chuckles roadmaps of whimsical chance.

Unanswered Prayers in Lightyears

I send my thoughts like rockets,
But they fizzle out in stardust,
My wishes echo through deep space,
Yet they vanish without a fuss.

I ask for love from comets bright,
They just zoom past, what a sight!
Orbs of gas, they laugh and sway,
While I beg for a sign to stay.

Oh planets, could you take a note?
My hopes float by like a fluffy boat,
But they chuckle in rings of dust,
While I ponder in cosmic trust.

So here I am, a cosmic clown,
With dreams that fly, but don't come down,
In this endless dance, I still am found,
While stars roll their eyes all around.

The Cosmic Dissonance of Heart and Sky

I shout my love to distant stars,
But they dance like they're at bars,
Awkward hugs from galaxies far,
My heart's a DJ, spinning bizarre.

Wishing on a meteor's tail,
Yet it trips over some cosmic veil,
My heart beats loud, the stars roll their eyes,
As they guffaw at my heartfelt sighs.

The Milky Way's a safety net,
But it's never caught my sunset,
Cosmic problems, I'm in the mix,
While stardust giggles at my fix.

So I twirl under the void's gaze,
Feeling like a clown in a cosmic maze,
With a heart that's lost and still believes,
That someday, love's the one that weaves.

When Nightfall Brings Only Silence

I wish upon a twinkling light,
But no one answers in the night,
The crickets chirp a lonely tune,
While I chat with the lazy moon.

My secrets drift to stardust dust,
The darkness grins, says, "In you I trust!"
But faith's a prankster, laughs with glee,
While I'm talking to a galaxy.

The meteors pass as I confess,
Yet they just giggle, I must digress,
Shooting stars, it seems, have bad brains,
While I linger in cosmic lanes.

So I'll sit with my silent wish,
Whispers caught in the vast abyss,
A jester lost in space's play,
As night yawns and steals my say.

Constellations Watching Over Wistfulness

Up above, they twinkle, mock my plea,
Constellations rolling in glee,
With shapes so funny and grand designs,
While I craft heart-shaped stars for signs.

The Bear's a prankster, sly and strange,
It buoys my hopes, just to derange,
As Orion winks, the night's bestmate,
And I wonder if they think I'm great.

My dreams fling high, but hit a wall,
Like comets too busy to call,
Starlit guardians, with laughter to share,
Just remind me, they just don't care.

On this strange ride of light and dark,
Each blink's a giggle, a silly spark,
But here I remain, a joyous soul,
Under cosmic jokes, I still feel whole.

The Cosmic Irony of Solitary Cries

In the vastness I shout, my voice echoes wide,
Yet the stars just twinkle, with nothing to bide.
They dance in their silence, a radiant tease,
While I'm here on my own, begging for ease.

I try to converse with a comet or two,
But they zoom right past me, like they never knew.
It's cosmic comedy, my plight unfolds,
As I laugh at the space where my wishes are told.

A moonbeam winks at me, what a cruel jest!
It's hard to keep humor when you're feeling less blessed.
I wave at the planets, they only just spin,
As if my grand wishes are a joke to begin.

So here I remain, a lone cosmic fool,
In this great endless space, I'm breaking the rule.
I shout into starlight, but all I can see,
Is the punchline of humor, and it's just me!

A Celestial Canvas Painted in Solitude

On this canvas of black, I paint my desires,
Each stroke met with silence, like unsung choirs.
Planets wheel past, with a nonchalant flair,
While I stand in awe, whispering to air.

My brush dipped in hope, I color the night,
Yet the galaxies giggle and dim down their light.
It's a cosmic joke, I'm starting to see,
As I paint my grand dreams with an empty decree.

I sketch constellations, but they merely blink,
As if they're in on a joke, while I just sink.
Nothing but twinkling as answers return,
It's a galaxy's jest on a lonely concern.

So I'll laugh with this void, a charm in my heart,
A brush with the absurd, that's a stellar art.
In a space full of wonders, I find my delight,
In this cosmic canvas, painted in plight.

When Comets Bypass My Yearning

Oh comets of wonder, they flash and they zoom,
But they never stop by, just making me fume.
With tails like confetti, they burst from the dark,
While I stand here waiting, lost in the spark.

I raise up my hands, in a grand cosmic plea,
But they swerve around me, like bees around tea.
I'm left with no answers, just stardust and air,
As I ponder the humor of this cosmic affair.

Maybe one day, they'll pause in their flight,
And laugh at my yearnings under the moonlight.
Til then I'll keep wishing, with giggles and sighs,
As comets fly past, my hopes in disguise.

For who needs full answers when joy's in the chase?
With every bright flash, I'll just smile in space.
It's a whimsical dance, this celestial game,
With comets my jesters, oh isn't it lame?

The Unseen Symphony of Starry Night

In the quiet of night, I hum a soft tune,
But the stars seem to snicker, under the moon.
They twirl in a ballet, completely unfazed,
While I clatter my wishes, in a cosmic craze.

I conduct with my hands, waving high to the sky,
Yet the notes drift away, like a butterfly.
The planets keep spinning, in tight-lipped glee,
While I play solo, where's the harmony?

An orchestra's waiting, but they just won't play,
As I tap on the silence, hoping they'll stay.
The comets are coy, as they giggle and glide,
With an unseen symphony, I'm left to decide.

So I'll hum my tune loud, with whimsy in sight,
For the cosmos is playful, on this starry night.
With laughter and dreams, I'll embrace the unknown,
In the symphony's silence, I'll make it my own.

Threads of Thought in a Cosmic Nebula

In a nebula so bright, I shout,
But my words float out, like a kite in a drought.
Stars twinkle back, with laughter in sight,
Yet my cosmic jokes just don't feel quite right.

I ponder the void, like it's in on the game,
My thoughts spin like planets, but none know my name.
I wave to the comets as they zoom by in glee,
While they skip past my party, just not into me.

Galaxies swirl in a dance far from here,
But I bring the punchlines they don't want to hear.
I laugh at myself, in stellar despair,
Wishing for echoes in the cold cosmic air.

So I sit with my quirks, in a twinkly mess,
Crafting my lines, though they cause some distress.
With dreams of a cosmic audience so grand,
Still, no giggling stardust will lend me a hand.

Silent Responses of Distant Suns

Oh distant suns, do you hear my plea?
I've got comedy gold, just waiting for free!
But your bright beams of light just blink back at me,
Like I'm a mere shadow in a cosmic spree.

I try to impress with my stellar wit,
But your solar flares seem to not give a bit.
I juggle my thoughts in a galactic stand-up,
While your plasma shells bubble, in silent hiccup.

Nebulae giggle, while I tell my best joke,
Yet it feels like a punchline that's simply bespoke.
So I stare at the stars, in their shimmering fame,
Wishing they'd chuckle and join in the game.

But they twinkle and wink with indifference so high,
While I pitch cosmic tales that just flutter and die.
In this cosmic comedy, I float with my dreams,
Hoping for laughter from far-flung regimes.

The Parade of Stars, Unaware of Me

A parade of stars is marching along,
With glitters and glams, playing their song.
I wave from the sidelines, in hope to be seen,
But they strut past my spotlight, as though I'm unseen.

I crack a few jokes, in complete solitude,
But they just keep dancing, the glorious brood.
The comets refuse to twirl, give me a nudge,
While I'm left here grinning, just a party judge.

With planets in line, and bright asteroids,
I shout with enthusiasm, still no one enjoys.
The moon tries to smile, but turns out a frown,
I'm the lone cheerleader in this cosmic gown.

So I sit on the sidelines, laugh at my plight,
All the while stars twinkle, with pure delight.
In this cosmic parade, I seem to be lost,
A spectator, a dreamer, who's counting the frost.

When Celestial Bodies Stand Unmoved

When I speak to the planets, they don't flinch a hair,
As I deliver my lines, drifting out into air.
Stars look in my direction, yet avoid my fun,
It seems their attention is nowhere to run.

Venus yawns loudly, while Mars plays a tune,
I try to ignite a cosmic commune.
But they dance in their orbits, without any sound,
While I toss out my punchlines, falling unbound.

Saturn snorts laughter, but just won't engage,
With rings spinning round like the world's biggest stage.
I'm left with my quips, in a vast, empty space,
With comets that zoom past, not leaving a trace.

So I tiptoe along, with my hopes in a twist,
In the book of the stars, I just can't exist.
As I churn out my jokes, floating lost in the night,
Hoping one day they'll join, and my humor ignite.

Yearning for Echoes Among the Celestial

I shout to the stars bright,
But they just twinkle in flight.
My wishes float like balloons,
While silence dances to tunes.

Oh, moon, don't you hear my plea?
Or are you just sipping tea?
The planets roll their eyes wide,
As I ramble and bide my pride.

I send my words into the void,
Yet all I get is a dull noise.
Could it be I'm talking to air?
Or do comets just not care?

A cosmic joke played on me,
While asteroids giggle with glee.
I call to space, where echoes flee,
Yet I laugh—who needs reply, really?

Moments Lost in the Quiet Firmament

In the silence of the night,
I talk to stars, all so bright.
But they offer naught but winks,
As I ponder, and overthink.

Meteor showers, please respond,
Am I lost—are you still fond?
I cast my wishes up high,
But they just swirl, oh my, oh my!

A shooting star zips past me,
Wishing it would just agree.
But it's off on its own quest,
Leaving me, the cosmic jest.

I gossip with the Milky Way,
But it's busy, come what may.
While black holes do the cha-cha-cha,
Leaving me here, chaotically ajar.

A Heart Crying to the Celestial Silence

With a heart full of dreams loud,
I try to gather a crowd.
Yet the cosmos just yawns wide,
As my chatter drifts like a tide.

I pour my thoughts like stardust,
Yet silence seems the only must.
Galaxies spin and they mock,
While my words just tick-tock, tick-tock.

Why do stars always play shy?
They flash and shimmer, oh my, oh why?
I'm alone in this cosmic dance,
Hoping one will take a chance.

I send my heart across the void,
Yet my hopes, it feels, get destroyed.
With a laugh at the stellar fate,
I'll keep talking—can't wait, can't wait!

The Hidden Conversations Between Planets

Mercury whispers behind the sun,
While Venus just giggles for fun.
Earth is busy with its woes,
Mars is stuck in cosmic throes.

I try to eavesdrop on the chat,
But the silence is thick as a cat.
Jupiter spins tales of the past,
While Saturn just laughs, how long will it last?

Neptune hums a watery tune,
While thoughts drift like a cosmic balloon.
Pluto chimes in from afar,
Yet I'm here, wishing on a star.

Do planets ever hear my cheer?
Or are they too lost in their sphere?
I shout, but they just keep their beat,
While I ponder this dance of defeat.

Cosmic Lullabies to an Empty Sky

I sing soft songs to gentle night,
But stars just twinkle with pure delight.
My words float up, a feather's dream,
While silence reigns, or so it seems.

A comet zooms past with a glare,
I shout and wave, but it doesn't care.
Galaxies spin, each dance a tease,
While I'm left here, just counting fleas.

Oh moon, your shine is quite absurd,
Is anyone out there, have you heard?
I tap on hope with fingertips sweet,
But all I get is blankness, neat.

So I hum a tune to a bouncy star,
Thinking, surely, they'll hear from afar.
But stardust laughs in a cosmic joke,
And I stand lost, a lonely bloke.

Beneath a Canopy of Unacknowledged Dreams

Under this dome of cosmic delight,
I whisper wishes into the night.
But nearby planets just roll their eyes,
While comets traipse by in disguise.

I ponder the fate of my grand schemes,
As shooting stars dodge my hopeful beams.
The void echoes back, a silly jest,
Did I call for help? Or just a guest?

Oh black hole, you're a swirling mess,
You swallow my thoughts, I must confess.
I'd toss a prayer, but they're out of stock,
And my best friend, the moon, just mocks.

So I giggle loud at this cosmic ballet,
As dreams flop like fish in a cabaret.
Beneath this vast and empty dome,
I'm still here grinning, called it my home.

Unanswered Questions Beneath the Stars

I pose great queries to the night sky,
Like, why can't aliens just stop by?
But constellations just blink and yawn,
As I sit here in my pajamas at dawn.

Do stars have secrets they won't unveil?
Like, why do they twinkle? Or is that a tale?
With each failed answer, I raise a toast,
To the big, ol' cosmos, it loves to roast.

I ask for signs, perhaps a clue,
But stardust giggles, it's no déjà vu.
My mysteries swirl in a clumsy dance,
While the universe winks at my lack of chance.

Yet in this vastness, I still find glee,
A cosmic riddle, just you and me.
So I'll keep asking, with a laugh on my face,
In this silly game of galactic space.

The Light Years Between Us

There's light years stretched between us now,
Like cheese on a pizza; I wonder how.
My messages float, but they never arrive,
Just cosmic dust in a starry hive.

I send out signals, bright and clear,
But echoes return, and they disappear.
Oh planets, why won't you give a shout?
I swear I'm charming, without a doubt!

Aliens roaming, just out of reach,
I throw my best jokes, I try to teach.
But they seem busy, with their cosmic games,
While I'm just here, calling names.

So I laugh aloud, and raise my glass,
To the distant stars that I cannot harass.
In this playful void, I'll make my stand,
With humor my weapon, and dreams so grand.

Lament of the Cosmic Bystander

I shout at stars across the void,
They twinkle back but feel devoid.
My grand requests, they fade away,
It's hard to win when they're on play.

I dance for comets, wave my hands,
But they just glide through foreign lands.
My cosmic miming met with glee,
While black holes laugh, just not at me.

I send out notes in bottle-shaped ships,
Yet find my dreams on solar flips.
A crowd of nothing gathers near,
To witness my interstellar cheer.

So here I sit, in darkness long,
Creating verses, feeling wrong.
For all my flair, and dreams so bright,
I'm just a whisper in the night.

Messages Cast into the Infinite

I typed a wish on cosmic code,
Pressed send and watched my dreams explode.
Yet silence reigned, no thumbs-up cheer,
Did my Wi-Fi drop? Oh, dear, oh dear!

Signal lost in swirling dust,
Galaxies spread, but I can't trust.
Shooting stars just roll their eyes,
As I await my grand reply.

I scribble dreams on meteor trails,
But they dissolve like fishy tales.
"Send help!" I cry, to Mars, to space,
But they just float while I lose face.

I'll curl up small, make my own fun,
Pretend I'm winning, just for a run.
The cosmos grins, a cosmic tease,
While I chuckle at such whimsies.

When Planets Drift Unaware

I waved at Venus, oh look at her shine,
Yet she spun away, just sipping wine.
"Hey, Earth!" I called, with all my might,
But she was busy with pending night.

Jupiter shrugged, "It's not my day,"
As Saturn's rings twirled, in disarray.
My calls, it seems, just drift on by,
As stars blink twice, then go awry.

I wear a hat, to catch their glance,
Yet cosmic parties miss my dance.
Do black holes hide the best of joke?
I guess I'm just the punchline, broke.

Oh, let me laugh at my own plight,
As I throw confetti into the night.
For in this vast, unyielding sea,
Perhaps it's just me, a cosmic spree.

A Dialogue with the Unresponsive Night

I called to shadows, made my pitch,
But darkness just remained the niche.
"Can you hear my tales of woe?"
Yet silence answered, with a low.

I knocked on stars with pounding heart,
But they were busy, playing part.
"Hey, Milky Way, want to chat?"
But all I got was cosmic pat.

I sent my thoughts through nebulae,
Hoping they'd spark some witty reply.
Yet all I found were fleeting beams,
What is this? A cosmic theme?

So here I sit, with quirky jokes,
As meteors swirl amidst their hoax.
I'll share my dreams with the moonlight bright,
In my own space, I'll be polite.

How the Stars Forget My Name

I shouted at the sky today,
Hoping for a sign to stay.
But glittering dots, they just blinked,
Perhaps my words just stinked!

I wished upon a shooting star,
But it zips by, not quite ajar.
Is there a cosmic voicemail?
Or did my message simply fail?

The constellations dance and play,
While I'm here, they just sashay.
I'd complain, but who would care?
The stars just twinkle, unaware!

So here I sit, with dreams to share,
A cosmic chat, but all is air.
Maybe next time, I'll write in rhyme,
At least then, I'll have a good time!

Messages in an Empty Galaxy

I typed a note to galaxies far,
Hoping they'd reply with a star.
But silence greets my cosmic call,
Not even a chirp, not one at all!

I sent my thoughts on a comet's tail,
But it zoomed off like a speedy snail.
Were they too deep, my dreams of flight?
Or lost amidst the dark of night?

An interstellar chat would be grand,
If only space had a helping hand.
But space is busy – or so it seems,
While I'm just here, stuck with my dreams.

Perhaps I need a better tone,
A cosmic DJ with skills well-known.
For now, I'll laugh at my empty plea,
In this lonely, starry jubilee!

Beyond the Milky Way's Listening Ear

I often whisper to the black expanse,
Hoping for a cosmic dance.
But echoes blend in endless space,
Just my thoughts, with no embrace.

I imagined aliens, all with style,
To nod their heads and stay a while.
But they must be out grocery shopping,
While I stand here just non-stopping.

A supernova might hear my plight,
Blasting off into the cold, dark night.
Yet even they are far too bright,
To pay attention; no answers in sight!

Someday I'll get a reply, you'll see,
When a quasar finally thinks of me.
But for now, I'll pretend it's all a game,
And have a laugh at my lonely fame!

The Unheard Wishes of a Dreamer

I dreamt big dreams of spacey things,
Of giant ships and magic wings.
But when I wished, the silence grew,
And even the moonjust said, "Who?"

On a starlit night, I called for fate,
A cosmic buddy – oh, that'd be great!
But my hopes are lost in the cosmic sea,
Swallowed whole by apathy.

The planets spin, they laugh and swirl,
While I sit here, with a frown and twirl.
No postcards sent from Mars or home,
Just a riddle wrapped in stardust foam.

So to my dreams, I'll raise a toast,
For the empty wishes I love the most.
Though no one's listening, I'll sing out loud,
In this universe, I wear my proud!

The Weight of Words Untold Among Stars

I shout my dreams to the night sky,
Hoping the stars give them a try.
But they twinkle back like they're on break,
Leaving me wondering what's at stake.

My hopes float up, like balloons in a breeze,
But they drift away with incredible ease.
I guess the cosmos has better things,
Like swirling galaxies and cosmic flings.

I chat with comets, make witty quips,
While black holes just swallow my clever tips.
The moon's too busy with its own mood,
And the sun's shining bright, ignoring my brood.

So here I am with my voice in the void,
A cosmic comedian, quite overjoyed.
I'll keep talking, though they don't reply,
After all, space is a pretty funny guy!

Gazing Upward at Unforgiving Skies

I looked up once, saw a star so bright,
Decided to chat, thought it was polite.
But that star just flickered, played hard to get,
Leaving me hanging, quite the duet.

So I told the clouds, 'O fluffy white crew,
Let's have a party, just me and you!'
But they rained on my plans, didn't even respond,
Just floated by like a cosmic blonde.

I wrote a letter to the Milky Way,
Hoping it'd read, join the fun and play.
But it sent back silence, what a great friend!
Turns out the galaxies don't like to blend.

So I'll keep gazing at the skies above,
Hoping one day they'll show me some love.
But until then, I'll just laugh and say,
At least the stars don't care what I weigh!

The Emptiness of Cosmic Listening

I often wonder if they hear my pleas,
The meteors rushing like they've got keys.
I try to make sense of their silent dance,
But they twirl away, not a single glance.

I ask the planets, 'What's the secret code?'
They spin around, like they're on their own road.
Mars just waved, Venus rolled her eyes,
Leaving me baffled, oh what a surprise!

My words just echo in the great abyss,
Where asteroids chuckle at my cosmic miss.
I thought I'd found a friend in the moon,
But it just hummed a nonchalant tune.

Yet here I stand, chuckling at the plight,
A one-person show in the velvet night.
At least I've got jokes, and a heart full of glee,
In a galaxy where no one hears me!

Cosmic Canvas Dripping with Silence

Painting stars with hopes and dreams galore,
But they splatter back, leaving me wanting more.
My brush strokes falter, oh what a mess,
The sky's an artist, but won't confess.

I whispered to constellations, 'Join my art!'
But they just twinkled, playing hard to start.
'Why not a selfie?' I called through the night,
But they shifted away, not impressed by my sight.

I tried to tune in, hear their grand plan,
But it's all static—no way to understand.
The nebulas flicker, like they're in on a joke,
While I stand here wrapped in celestial cloak.

But I can't help but smile at this cosmic game,
A jester in space, with no one to blame.
For even in silence, I find my own cheer,
In this hilarious void, I've nothing to fear!

Echoes in the Void

I shout to the stars, they just blink and sway,
My hopes sail past, like a comet's stray.
I tap my forehead, they won't take the cue,
I guess I'll just laugh, at my cosmic boo-hoo.

In the vastness of space, I feel quite absurd,
Talking to stardust, but it won't say a word.
I throw out my wishes, they fizzle and pop,
Like balloons on a rocket, they fail to drop.

I ponder my fate with a wink and a grin,
Who needs a reply, when laughter's a win?
I'll serenade planets with all of my glee,
Why worry at all? They just don't care for me.

In cosmic confetti, I dance and I sing,
The black hole's my dance floor, I'm ready for bling.
Echoes of giggles travel light years away,
While I chat with my shadow, and joke all the day.

Stars Whispers Past My Thoughts

They sparkle above like they know my name,
But whispers of wisdom? Nah, they're lame.
I toss my confessions into the cosmic sea,
But they giggle and twinkle, ignoring poor me.

I send my best jokes to the Milky Way crew,
But they snicker in silence, like stars often do.
A light year away, they chuckle and beam,
While I sit on my couch, lost in a dream.

If planets could talk, oh the tales they'd share,
But all I receive is the cold, empty air.
I'll sip on my soda and wonder in jest,
Why I bother at all? I'm not their guest.

I'll play hide and seek with my thoughts in the night,
While they offer me nothing but pretty starlight.
So here's to my musings, all jumbled and wild,
To cosmic rejection, I still remain smiled.

Silent Conversations with Infinity

I lean on the edge of the infinite space,
Clutching my thoughts like they're part of the race.
Infinity winks, but it never replies,
I guess it's too busy with its billions of guys.

I talk to the moon about woes and delight,
But all I get back is a glow in the night.
Do craters have secrets? They seem pretty cool,
While I'm left down here, feeling like a fool.

I throw out my quirks, I parade my puns,
Yet the cosmos just twirls, dancing with suns.
I chase down my dreams, like comets in flight,
But they vanish like smoke in the quiet of night.

So here's to my chat with a silence so grand,
Where echoes of laughter just float in the sand.
I'll jest with the void, watch the time fly,
Who needs understanding? I can still wave goodbye.

Cosmic Murmurs and My Silent Pleas

I tossed a wish up, a gleaming delight,
But all that came back was a flicker of light.
I danced with the comets, I pranced 'round the stars,
Yet they just spin circles, in their cosmic cars.

I scribble my thoughts on a scrap of the night,
But they vanish like stardust, out of my sight.
I grin at the void, what more can I say?
It's totally chill, even when they decay.

With each little giggle, I pull up a chair,
To chat with the silence, without any care.
They pluck at my heartstrings, a celestial tease,
While I stew in my humor—oh, like a breeze!

So let's toast to the cosmos, my invisible friend,
Though silence reigns supreme, my antics won't end.
I'll throw all my banter into the vast sea,
And dream of the day one star talks back to me.

Cosmic Murmurs and My Silent Pleas

I whisper my hopes to the wide-open sky,
But the stars just chuckle, as they flicker by.
I send them my wishes, like messages sweet,
But all I receive is a silence complete.

Galaxies spin as I plead and I pine,
They twirl and they dance, but their hearts are so fine.
I guess I'm just one in a gajillion dreams,
While they twinkle above, plotting their schemes.

I shout my confessions to black holes so deep,
But my secrets dissolve, like wishes on sheep.
If only they'd text me, just once for a laugh,
But the whispers of cosmos keep me in the half.

With humor my shield and a smile on my face,
I chat with the stardust, keeping up with the pace.
And though I may never find answers or peace,
I'll live for the giggles, a cosmic release.

The Indifference of Celestial Bodies

Stars spin and twinkle, heads in the clouds,
They laugh at my wishes, mocking my shrouds.
I shout at the moon, it just grins with delight,
While comets fly past, they ignore my plight.

Galaxies swirl, with secrets to keep,
They're busy aligning, and I can't get any sleep.
I toss my dreams upward, hoping for fate,
But dark matter chuckles, "We're never too late!"

Black holes are swirling, they've turned off their phones,
As I ponder my life, I feel so alone.
I ask for a sign, preferably bright,
But they're all out partying, just out of sight.

Yet still I keep yelling, for laughter, I plead,
Perhaps I'll get noticed, maybe they'll heed.
For cosmic confusion is laughter in space,
And maybe one day, I'll get embraced.

Lost in Translation Among the Celestials

I sent a postcard to the stars up high,
But it got lost in space, oh me, oh my!
They must have read it, in some other tongue,
As meteors pass, keeping their song unsung.

Venus keeps blushing while I fumble my lines,
Jupiter's swirling, busy with his designs.
With every attempt, my words get more frail,
Even Mars is snickering, "You're doomed to fail!"

I try to decode constellations in flight,
But Orion just chuckles, "You're not quite right!"
Translation's a puzzle too complex for me,
As the cosmos rolls on in a cosmic spree.

Who knew that starlight could be such a tease?
I laugh with the planets, they're hard to appease.
For every attempt at connection I make,
The silence from stardust gives me a break!

The Solitude of a Cosmic Heart

I wear my heart cosmic, a spark in the void,
But it feels overlooked, maybe a bit toyed.
I wave at the planets, they just look away,
While black holes engulf all that I want to say.

Shooting stars zoom past, with wishes to spare,
But I'm stuck on the ground, in my own little snare.
The comets zoom by with their cosmic flair,
While I'm here on Earth, like I'm just not there.

Perhaps I'll throw confetti to the Milky Way,
In hopes that my feelings might catch them today.
A picnic on Pluto, oh what a thought,
But no one shows up, I feel quite distraught.

Yet laughter erupts in the silence so grand,
As I keep on dancing, my heart in my hand.
For solitude's humor is a delightful game,
And I'll keep on reaching, no matter how lame.

Cosmic Questions Without Answers

Why do the stars seem to giggle at night?
As I ask all my questions, they twinkle with light.
I ponder and ponder, what's the deal with the void?
Why's cosmic wisdom so often avoided?

Why can't I touch a nebula's veil?
Instead, all I feel is a soft cosmic gale.
I chase after answers, while asteroids tease,
Ignoring my queries like a cosmic breeze.

Are aliens laughing at all of my fears?
Or just sipping stardust, shedding their tears?
I send them my thoughts through my flimsy old phone,
But they're busy exploring, so I'm all alone.

Yet questions keep flowing like rivers of light,
With each cosmic laugh, I find joy in the fight.
For mysteries linger, and stars spark my dreams,
In the grand cosmic puzzle, nothing's as it seems.

www.ingramcontent.com/pod-product-compliance
Lightning Source LLC
Chambersburg PA
CBHW072135070526
44585CB00016B/1682